This Journal Belongs To:

Made in the USA
Middletown, DE
31 May 2022

66473138R00066